HIGH COUNTRY CANVAS

HIGH COUNTRY CANVAS

by Vada F. Carlson

Illustrations by Joe Rodriguez

NORTHLAND PRESS

This book
is lovingly dedicated
to all those relatives
and friends
who have given us inspiration
and courage
throughout the years.

CONTENTS

High Country Canvas 2
At Summer's Ending 4
Chiaroscuro 6
Dust Storm in Navajoland 8
In Defense of Mesas 10
Strange Trinity 12
Prairie Tramp 14
Witch Wind 16
The Mexican, the Burro,
  and the Bell 18
Nostalgia 20
Desert Treasure 22
Provision 24
Lizard Beware 26
The Old Buck 28
Acknowledgment 30
All Else Is Still 32
Autumn Fancy 34
War Bonnet Sunset 36

At Mt. Rushmore
  — 2954 A.D. 38
Navajo Way 40
My Soul Was a Sailor 42
Desert Picture 44
So Runs the River 46
Waddy's Lament 48
Acceptance 50
These Are the Tetons 52
The Desert Speaks 54
Prune Well the Vine 56
Indigo Bush 58
Mother Instinct 60
Adobe Walls 62
Canyon de Chelly 64
Wish 66
Wings of Time 68
Now, I Remember 70
Prairie March 72

Spearthrust 74

Dig Down 76

Teach Them, O Lord 78

Definition 80

The Mountains Are Monks 82

Chinde 84

Cycle 86

Reminder 88

Prescience 90

Wind: Desert Sculptor 92

Grace Notes 94

Predestined 96

My Baby Sleeps 98

Harvesters 100

High Country Canvas

White are the stern, towering slopes of the Peaks,
    Vividly green is the forest below,
Deep red the cinders that carpet the flat
    Where sweet-scented pinyons and junipers grow.

Silent the scene till the pinyon jays come,
    Saucy, blue-feathered, with never a care,
To eat the brown nuts and blue juniper berries
    That headline the forest cafe's bill of fare.

At Summer's Ending

All unaware of summer's ending,
The pampered cows,
Quiescent, drowse
On beds of sun-warmed purple clover,
Or idly browse
Along the cattailed edges
Of the meadow pool
That mirrors storm clouds drifting over
And ragged, wavering wedges
Of gabbling geese —
No beat of wild blood giving them a reason
To note the symbols of the changing season:
Storm clouds flying, cattails bending,
Wild geese crying summer's ending.

Chiaroscuro

Somewhere within this shaggy house of sullen sod,
This ebon blot against the silver drift of hills,
Its windows small, deep-set, like weary, dim old eyes
Reflecting, now, the chaste white light of winter skies,
A woman kneels.

A woman kneels,
And never feels black shadows pressing, pushing in;
White as her hair and gown, she bears no weight of sin;
Her soul a still, pale pool of peace, contentment fills.

In prayer, she shares the moonlit solitude with God.

6

Dust Storm
in Navajoland

This is a night when the spirits walk,
Shrieking and wailing,
Wrapped around
With dusty blankets
Torn from the ground.

Crouch on your sheepskins;
Do not talk;
This is a night when the spirits walk.

In Defense of Mesas

"A bitter land, and bleak,"
  They say, and hasten on,
  Drenching the rare, pine-scented air
  With gasoline.
  They have not seen the tender green
  Upon the sage,
  Nor glimpsed the wax fragility of cactus bloom.

Strange Trinity

A hillside rises steeply from this trail,
First marked by some old padre's patient tread,
And halfway up the slope, a weathered cross
Establishes a homesite of the dead.
Beside the grave, a patch of prickly pear
Sprawls as it did a century ago,
When that proud caballero was alive
And master of the valley down below.

The crumbling 'dobe his hands helped to build
Contains no evidence of how he died;
But she for whom his life was forfeited
Does not, in death, lie resting by his side.
All is forgotten now . . . the love . . . the hate . . .
The blazing passions and resulting loss;
All that remains is this strange trinity
Of trail, and piercing thorn and weathered cross.

Prairie Tramp

Unlike the cultivated, pampered rose,
The tumbleweed must grow, unsupervised;
It thrusts its slender root down where it may
And, by some strength its nature has devised,
The dauntless weed
Brings forth its bristling branches,
Flowers and seed.

Its cycle run, the prairie tramp lets go
Its hold upon the parent earth and heeds
The long-resisted wooing of the wind . . .
And in its awkward flight arouses needs
In us to be
As wondrously sufficient —
And as free.

Witch Wind

Fearful the fox in the rabbit brush;
Cautious the coyote, deep in his den;
Still as a shadow the shy brown thrush;
Crouched in her nest the cactus wren;
Saved, one and all, by their chosen shields,
From the sandy whip the Witch-Wind wields.

The Mexican,
the Burro, and
the Bell

In San Ramón tree shadows laced the field
Where one lone farmer with his burro plowed,
Preparing dormant soil for summer's yield
While mourners straggled up a cobbled street
And church bells bonged. The burro flapped its ears,
The farmer, black head bent, gaze on bare feet,
Paused long enough to cross himself, and then
Continued down the furrow, for his corn
Was waiting to be buried in the earth,
To lose identity, and live again.

He sensed the miracle in this rebirth.
The burro plodded on; the bronze bells bonged.

Nostalgia

She could not understand her husband's quiet joy
In jagged peaks that stabbed the sunset sky,
For she was sandhill born, had ever known and loved
Low sandy hills that stood like friends, close by.
Dismayed, she gazed into the purpling distances
That yawned beyond the miles of brooding sage,
While in her heart there burned a flame of loneliness
That only friendly sandhills could assuage.

Desert Treasure

Each day the setting sun unlocks
The desert's treasure chest, and spills
Gold dust along eroded hills.
And, as it gilds the mesa rocks,
It turns the cholla's barbed defense
Into a haloed innocence.

With coral, then with amethyst,
The desert buttes in turn are draped;
Where rocks by wind and rain are shaped,
And arid washes wind and twist
Like snakes across the sun-baked land
More gold is flung with lavish hand.

For strangers, who prefer to feast
Their eyes on less flamboyant fare
Than clouds of flame and topaz, there
Is turquoise sky and opal east . . .
But while a jewel's left in the chest
True desert lovers face the west.

Provision

No doubt the questing wild birds never know
That God's divine provision for such things
As restless wings
Includes the possibility of snow;
That He anticipates their future needs
By packing seeds
Into the cupboards of the wayside weeds,
While days are sunny and the nights are warm,
And there's no slightest hint of winter storm.
Serene, the birds fly off into the blue
To wing the trackless highways of the sky,
Till by and by
The gray days come, as gray days always do;
Then, quite undaunted by the snowy pall
That covers all,
They spy the wayside weeds, so gaunt and tall,
And clustering on them till the full heads nod,
They take provision from the hand of God.

Lizard, Beware!

O, lizard, beware!
You're as quick as a wink
But not as immune
From attack as you think.
Don't lie in the sun
Puffed up in your pride
Till a chaparral cock
Neatly punctures your hide.
Your body, my friend,
He will coldly impale
With a jab of his beak
And a flirt of his tail.
If you have a fear
You're wise not to lull it,
Lest you disappear
Down a roadrunner's gullet.

The Old Buck

The old buck, trembling, bloody, nearly spent,
Paused on the mountain trail to sniff the breeze,
And found it redolent of lion scent —
A warning he must seek the shade and freeze.
His yearlings and the does of his delight
Were feeding in the meadow down below,
As placidly as though he'd won the fight
Conceded to the younger buck, his foe.
His eyes were glazing as he turned to meet
The lion, glaring at him from the trail;
A beast that stalked him, now, on padded feet;
A yellow Death with fangs and lashing tail.

The lion snarled, and sprang to make the kill;
The young buck led his prizes down the hill.

Acknowledgment

I thank Thee, Lord, that I have seen the rosy glow
    Of rising winter sun on virgin snow;
That I have seen the ebon sky on moonless nights
    Pulse with the far stars' unimpassioned lights,
While ever-restless winds, in mood benign,
    Caressed the topmost branches of a pine.
I thank Thee, Lord, that I have heard the nightbird's call
    Above the frenzy of a waterfall;
That I have lived, before my earthly work was done,
    Where cedars swelter in the summer sun,
And that Thy storms reveal, after their bitter rage,
    The heady fragrance of the twisted sage.

All Else Is Still

A nighthawk dips and soars on spotted wings,
      Serene and strong;
Far up the trail a lonely coyote sings
      His evening song,
      Then all is still
Except for gentle whispers from the trees
      That climb the hill.
The soft west wind bears in her arms the deep
      Sweet tang of pine,
And darkness wakes a trillion stars to leap
      And throb and shine.

      Atop the hill
The mournful pines are sighing in the breeze . . .
      All else is still.

Autumn Fancy

The sun is pouring down
From a sky of azure blue
And flooding hill and plain
With its bronzy-golden hue,
While from the west a breeze,
Idly drifting by,
Lifts a white aster's fringe,
Whispering, " Frost is nigh."

Too proud, the scarlet vines,
To droop and show their fears,
But all the cottonwoods
Are shedding golden tears.

War Bonnet Sunset

Who has seen glory to vie with a sunset —
a wild, western sunset; a war bonnet sunset,
with great, gaudy feathers of light
fanning up from the white, snarling teeth
of the peaks to the blue of the zenith;
a war bonnet sunset that lingers in loveliness
long after coppers and golds have been fused and forgotten;
that stands in the west as a chieftain,
with brightly dyed feathers of eagles
encircling his head, might have stood
long ago on a hilltop, facing the east
and beseeching his god, the Great Spirit,
to lead him, tomorrow, in victory home from the battle?

At Mt. Rushmore — 2954 A.D.

Fright held them speechless when they saw the head,
The massive features carved from solid stone
There on the mountainside — a lone
Reminder of a people lost and dead.
There had been others; noses, mouths and eyes
Lay strewn like bones upon the talus slopes,
And in their shattered silence spoke of hopes
The ancient ones had failed to realize.
The man stared at the Face; his hairy hand
More firmly clutched his club. His mate looked on
And marveled that he tried to understand
Where those who carved the heads from stone had gone.
Then slowly in them both a sadness grew.
They wept . . . for whom, for what, they never knew.

Navajo Way

Run ! . . . Run to the shelter,
The hogan, the haven,
And make your hearts good,
One toward another,
In the Navajo way,
For Storm God is coming.
    Snake tongues of fire
    He will dart from the heavens;
    But the truth of the Navajo Way
    Will protect you.

La ! . . . He is helpless !
See how the pink sand
Is drinking his bright silver tears ?

My Soul
Was A Sailor

I've but to see a painted beach
That painted waves race in to reach,
And I, who've never been to sea,
Feel fathoms surging under me,
Taste salty spray upon my lips
And hear the bellowing of ships.

In some "before" my soul has had,
It was, I'm sure, a sailor lad.

42

Desert Picture

We paused in desert loneliness to view
Red canyons, scrubby growth and painted sand,
And wondered, as so many travelers do,
How Navajos survive on such poor land.
Announced by silver tinkling of a bell
A band of sheep poured from a little draw,
And, herding them, a white lamb in her arms,
A child approached, to stare in solemn awe.

    This living picture I shall always keep:
    The desert child, her lamb, the herd of sheep.

So Runs the River

As music flows through unresisting air
In streams of beauty,
Unaware of human thought
Behind the placing of each note
In harmony for instrument and throat,
So runs the river to the restless sea,
To lose in salt its own identity.

Forgotten, in the land-assaulting tide,
Its rocky bed, the walls that served as guide.

Between the walls of self a mighty surge
Of formless Being,
Flowing free, awaits the urge
Of Mind to grasp and understand
The power, unlimited, at its command.

Waddy's Lament

When drifts in the gullies are melting
And spring's rolling over the hill
With mornings as clear as a whistle
Yet chuck full of snap and of chill,
I awake with each day's vivid dawning
Rowelled raw with a fevered desire
For a good drink of alkali water
And the smell of a sagebrush fire.

When the new grass is lush in the valleys
Where white-faces drowse in the sun,
When wildflowers abloom 'mid the sagebrush
Are proof that our summer's begun,
I chafe for my chaps and my saddle
And a cayuse hard ridin' won't tire —
Plus a good swig of alkali water
And the smell of a sagebrush fire.

You can say what you want about Heaven,
And harp of the joy that's to come,
But now me, I'm a hardboiled old waddy
And easier to please than some,
And They'll satisfy all of my yearnings,
All my soul's deep-branded desire,
If They'll stake me to alkali water
And a clear-burning sagebrush fire.

Oh, I'm homesick for alkali water
And the smell of a sagebrush fire,
For the bawlin' and snorts of the cow brutes
A'slakin' their thirst in the mire,
For the crazy yap-yappin' of coyotes
As the sun slips over the hill,
And the peace of a twilight that lingers
While the world sits perfectly still.

Acceptance

Emerging from beneath snow-weighted wings
Of hillside sage,
The lone cock pheasant pauses to survey
The blizzard's alteration of his world.
The storm's cold rage
Still threatens; sullen, low, the clouds of gray;
White lies the snow, a gravecloth on the field
Where he has fed.

With pinions whistling he lifts in flight;
His outthrust head
A living, vivid arrowpoint of red,
He hurtles through the chill air to alight
In snow; along the ice-locked larder
Of a buried ditch
He runs, accepting fate, his footsteps proud,
To decorate the soft folds of the shroud
In featherstitch.

These Are the Tetons

These are the Tetons;
Mighty mother symbols of the West
From whose artesian founts
True beauty flows;
He who has drunk from mirrored mounts
His greedy fill
Appreciates a hungry infant's thrill
When warm milk issues from the tapered breast
To which its seeking lips are firmly pressed.

The Desert Speaks

The desert speaks
In forests, prone and turned to stone,
Their length and girth
As brightly hued as painted earth;
In mesas, high in turquoise sky,
Where Hopis dwell
And ancient gods still weave their spell.

The desert speaks
In fleecy towers of clouds, and hours
Of silver rain
That briefly wets the parched terrain;
In golden days and easy ways
Of desert born;
In ebon night and crimson morn.

The desert speaks
In sunset fire on butte and spire;
In canyons carved
From rainbow soil; in stunted, starved
Persistent trees: In all of these
One hears its voice
And, having heard, stays on by choice.

Prune Well the Vine

Prune well the vine of thought
Where old ideas grew
And ripening, were harvested and pressed
Into the heady wine
Of visible accomplishment.

Prune well the waiting vine
For through this action new
Ideas sprout, mature, and are expressed,
Each in its true design.

This is the nature of the vine;
For this the vine was meant.

Indigo Bush

Beside the desert road, a shaggy bush,
Ignored by thousands and admired by none,
Grows meekly until April comes, and some
Perceptive souls arrive.
Then like a fairy princess, long bewitched,
Touched by a wand, finds freedom from her spell,
A force within the bush begins to swell
And from each dusty twig
Burst airy blooms of deepest indigo,
As though to prove how loving is a God
Who builds into each plant, each stone, each clod,
A beauty all its own.

Mother Instinct

I vowed I'd have no "bum" lambs in *my* kitchen,
Until that day I found you cold and still
Beside the lifeless body of your mother.
Newborn, untended in that lethal chill,
I knew you, too, would die, unless another
Took up your mother's task and scrubbed your pelt
With motherly insistence, till some inner
Spark was fanned, some primal urge was felt,
To make you struggle up and seek your dinner.
Forgetting what I'd vowed I snugly wrapped you
In gunnysacks, and racing through the storm
I found a "bum" lamb had become the center
Of my existence, and the goal my warm
Life-giving room I'd sworn you'd never enter.

Adobe Walls

There's no dissembling in adobe walls;
Dirt they were and dirt they will remain,
Yet in their humble strength
They stand in dignity upon the sunbaked plain,
As though in gratitude
To men whose calloused hands
First formed the ragged bricks
And built of them an earthy sacristy
For treasures held most dear.

For centuries they've borne with placid mien
The buffeting of desert winds and rains,
To separate the closely pressing grains
Whose purpose seems to be
To give them back to earth,
Where they may wait another million years
For men to see their worth.

Canyon de Chelly

A single grain of sand, alone,
Though it were blown by Heaven's mightiest gale,
Must surely fail to leave a scratch to catch
Man's eye, that he might trace its race
Along these glowering walls of stone;
Yet, wielded by the Master Sculptor's hand,
Small grains of sand, combined, had power to hew
This canyon through the sullen rough red stuff:

Man, too, if only he could see,
Like sand, cuts canyons through his land.

Wish

I shall not even wish to be
    As valiant as this storm-scarred tree,
Serene through bitter years,
    But just to be, when days are dark,
As plucky as the frightened lark
    That sings to quell its fears.

Wings of Time

Across the desert's bluebird sky,
    Like homing birds,
    In flight,
    The hours wing by.
    Dove dawn . . . Canary noon . . .
    Red robin sunset . . .
Then starling night.

Now, I Remember

Now, I remember
The eerie silence of the night,
Before the wind ran sighing and prying along the eaves;
And how like the sound of a band of sheep, rising in fright,
Was the whisper, the stir, then the sussurant scurry
        of cottonwood leaves.

Now, I recall
How my windows rattled as cold air probed,
And how the old house was shaken and buffeted by the storm . . .
Strange that this morning, with all the world fluffily robed,
Our snowbound harbor should be so comfortable and so warm.

But, now I remember
This is December.

Prairie March

Purple shadows on the bluffs,
Blue skies overhead,
Color in the landscape
That has been so cold and dead;
Water rushing down the gulch
Rag-tag drifts of snow,
Blackbirds in the cottonwoods
Telling all they know.
Over all the smell of Spring:
New turned sod and sage;
Nature's written Winter off,
And turned a clean brown page.

Spearthrust

Cart wheels creaked,
Oxen strained,
Strong men pushed . . .

The first brave trickle
Of seeking people
Crossed the river.

For them, this was a beginning:
A beginning of new life,
Freedom and hope.

Unseen, Apache braves
Observed this spearthrust
From the South.

That night the tom-toms thumped
And war cries rose
In a wild crescendo
Of futile protest.

For them, this was an ending:
An ending of unchallenged rule
And a beginning of struggle,
Bloodshed and despair.

Symbols of an era's beginning,
Another's ending:
The weathered *carreta* . . .
The Apache spear.

Dig Down

Plant trustfully your seed of good;
    Tend lovingly the tender shoot;
Give thanks for bud, for brilliant flower;
    For foliage and ripened fruit.

Nor think, when this one plant shall wilt,
    The good that was your joy has died:
Rejoice! Give thanks! Dig down and find
    Corms for new plantings multiplied.

Teach Them, O Lord

We pray Thee, Father, for a world at peace
Where we, your children, need no longer quail
At thought of gunfire and its lethal hail,
While vainly hoping warfare soon may cease.

We pray that someday we may know release
From soul-corroding hatreds that assail
Our daily lives. Let brotherhood prevail;
Let Love, throughout the Universe, increase.

Like drunken gamblers using living dice —
Those precious lives that cannot be restored —
The warring nations offer sacrifice.
O may Thy healing harmony be poured
On those who wage their wars at such a price.
Teach them, O Lord, to lay aside the sword.

Definition

Fortune's defined in various ways:
      In terms of mines and cattle,
      In cotton bales, tobacco sales,
      In stocks and bonds, and chattel.
      In jewels worthy of a crown,
      In mansions proud and regal,
      Perhaps as coveted renown,
      Though gained by means illegal.

But he who's felt the touch of Death
Knows Fortune means just one thing — Breath!

The Mountains Are Monks

The mountains are monks
With cowls on their heads
And snow mantles,
Touched with sun's gold,
On their shoulders.

Foothills crouch at their feet,
Their bare brown backs
Eternally bent in homage.

Chinde*

Touch me not,
For I am chinde . . . chinde !
Inside of me
My heart lies dead;
He whom I love
Has fled,
My body houses the dead . . .
Dead dreams . . . dead love.
Look not at me
And touch me not,
For I am chinde . . .
Chinde.

* Navajos believe a dead thing is taboo, or chinde.

Cycle

Our choice profundities another mouth will word:
The sounds we hear have been, before us, heard.
Sweet secrets, meant to thrill our hearts alone,
Beyond the reach of memory have been known
To other senses that have lived, and loved, and gone;
They will be known to others following on.

Eternally, from minimum to magnitude,
The widening ripples run. Fair flowers exude
Their priceless perfumes lavishly, then wilt and die.
And, dying, see their sweetness multiply,
As songs, long sung, become a part of Life's refrain,
An ancient echo, audible again.

Reminder

When snow is piled, marshmallow-white
    And light
As eiderdown on post and weed,
    We need
The incense found in good
    Hard wood,
The cheer that's in an oak log's blaze
    To raise
New hope. Remembering
    That spring's
Largess depends upon the snow,
    We know —
With grateful hearts and waning fear —
    Snow is His promise of a good New Year.

Prescience

Beyond my window, buntings search the weeds,
    Exploring hopefully for clinging seeds,
And one, enthralled, regards a fallen feather
    As though, despite this most inclement weather,
She feels Spring's urge, and dimly knows its needs.

Wind: Desert Sculptor

Knowing the waves he has carved cannot float
Iceberg or buoy or fisherman's boat;
Knowing no delicate fins will be fanned
Deep in those ripples of newly etched sand;
Certain, instead, they'll remain the abode
Of roadrunner, lizard, sidewinder, horned toad;
Wind, the old sculptor, pipes nautical tunes
While creating a masterpiece, out on the dunes.

Grace Notes

Above the mountain symphony:
      Percussive thunder of the falls,
      Throbbing harp strings of the stream,
      Wind's obbligato in the pines,
A feathered flutist's harmony
Repeats the major theme.

Predestined

Can Poetry survive ? . . . Ah, yes, it never dies;
Though blank the page, it lives. It lives
In skies where bird wings swoop and sweep;
In pulsing rhythms of the deep old sea;
Its memory endures from age to age.

Man's concept of the truth may change in varied ways,
Yet the strange and hidden cadence of the heart,
The tides, the nights, the days . . . each is a part
Of song and poetry.

Forever minds will grope until they reach
Kaleidoscopic shallows of the beach
Of Imagery,
And scout the shore
Until they find the store
Of universal poetry,
Alive,
Predestined to survive.

My Baby Sleeps

Hush !
Howl not in the rocks tonight,
Little gray brother.
And wind, whisper when you try my hogan door,
For my baby sleeps.

Thunder, growl not in the desert sky;
Fall gently, rain,
For my baby sleeps.

Beneath the smoke hole of my hogan,
Juniper, burn brightly,
And keep him warm —
My baby, my newborn son.

Harvesters

Blue as the blush on the juniper berries,
Pinyon jays wing where low evergreens grow,
Harvesting crops they've a duty to harvest
Quickly, before there's a deep fall of snow.

Sociably chattering, flashing blue feathers,
Confident, saucy, the travelers feed. . . .
Sweet are the nuts in their rusty brown covers,
Juicy the berries. . . . The pinyon jays heed
Instinct alone, for as harvesters reason,
Crops have one need ! To be gleaned in their season.

100